DECIDE

"A 6 Step Behavior Management Methodology that works!"

Kim Martin

To my amazing husband Joe and our children. To my
awesome Curves sisters, who have given me the experience
of coaching over the last 20 years and the inspiration for
me to develop the DECIDE method and write this book.

Kim Martin

CONTENTS

INTRODUCTION

DECIDE

How many times have you set out to achieve a goal, kick a bad habit, get healthy, be more organized, finish school, or learn something new, only to end up disappointed and unsuccessful? Like most people, you probably find it difficult to stay motivated or find the right resources to help you stay on track. You muster up the motivation to get started, but once an obstacle pops up, life stresses happen, or the excitement wears off, and you are back to ground zero.

You are not alone!

Statistically, 62% of people set goals, especially around the New Year. The other 38% don't set goals or make New Year's resolutions at all. (On a side note, I would argue for those who don't. It's most likely because they have never been successful in achieving goals and have given up altogether.) Out of the 62% of people who have goals, only 8% of them are ultimately successful in achieving them.

Where do you fall in this statistic? Are you one of the 62% of people who set goals, or have you given up altogether and no longer even concern yourself with goals because of experiencing failures in the past? Are you a part of the small percentage who has successfully completed your goals or the astounding 92% who hasn't?

I have great news for you! No matter where you align in the statistic, you *can* be successful in achieving your goals. If you have never succeeded before, I will teach you in this book how to change the behaviors that have held you back. If you are a goal setter but just can't seem to stay focused long enough to achieve your goal, you can be successful! If you are one of the 8% who experience success in achieving your goals, this book will help you break through your comfort zone and move up to the next level of success.

1. YOU MUST DECIDE

What is it that you want to do? What do you really want?

Let's dream for a moment...

Do you want to live a healthy lifestyle and kick some bad habits? Maybe run your first 5K or take up cycling? How about finish school and earn a college degree? You could be your own boss and start a business, change careers, be a better employee, write a book, get out of debt, go to church, or be a better friend, spouse, parent or child. Are you ready to start a family, have a baby, homeschool your kids, or get more involved? You could volunteer, give back to your community, or start a program that would help others. How about becoming organized and getting rid of excess clutter in your home or in your mind? Would you like to be more patient, less angry, happier, and grateful?

Whatever it is you want to do and whatever your dreams are ... You were born for success and you can do it!

With the right mindset, you can successfully achieve your goals and dreams. I refer to it as an "I've Decided" mindset. Most of us are caught up in an "I'll Try" mindset, which produces superficial goals like resolutions we never see come to fruition. A common phrase for those with an "I'll Try" mindset is, "I want it so bad, why is it so hard?" Have you ever said to yourself, "Why is it so hard if I want it so bad?" I know I have, and I have heard thousands of others whom I have coached over the past 20 years say it too!

Whatever it is you want to do and whatever your dreams are … You were born for success! How do I know this? The Lord says so!

"For I know the plans I have for you," declares the Lord, "plans to prosper you and not to harm you, plans to give you a hope and a future." - Jerimiah 29:11 (NIV)

Twelve years ago, I became a runner. You may ask, how did you become a runner? Well, I simply started running. It's true! Out of the blue, a friend of mine (I'll call her Mary for this book) asked me to run a two-mile fun run with her. I am relatively sure that at that time I had never even walked two miles consistently without stopping much less ran two miles, but it seemed like a good challenge and, of course, I wanted to support Mary. I will never forget the first time we went out to practice this new idea of running. I literally made it from my mailbox to the next mailbox on our street (which was about fifty feet at best) before I had to stop and walk. My first thoughts were, "I can't run. I am not a runner. I can't even breathe. I'm gasping for air." Luckily, Mary was with me, and although she was feeling the same defeat, her mindset was different. Mary was determined. She had DECIDED that she was going to run, no matter what. Mary had already signed up for the two-mile fun run, and her mindset was completely different than mine. Mary had decided, and I was riding the curtails of her decision. Lucky me! (On a side note, this is proof that the people you hang around with have a huge influence on what you decide to do or where you decide to go. We'll come back to that later.)

Not only did I complete that two miles, but since the start of my running career twelve years ago, I have run five marathons, at least ten half marathons, and countless other races. All of this happened because Mary decided to run two miles, and I decided to join her. I became a runner because I began to run.

"To become, you have to begin." This statement is a truism at its finest!

To be a runner, you simply need to start running. To fulfill a goal or a dream, you simply need to begin with the first step.

Since I am a runner, I love to use the analogy of running a marathon in comparison to achieving goals, dreams, or desires. I believe it is a correlation that almost everyone can conceptualize. Even if you have never run a mile in your life, it shouldn't be too difficult for you to imagine the dedication, time, discipline, accountability, and overall effort it takes to successfully complete a marathon. It should be relatively easy for you to understand that wanting to run a marathon is not enough to successfully complete a marathon. You could walk around for the rest of your life dreaming about it, wanting it more than anything, coveting other runners, going to every local race, and cheering on the sidelines. You could talk about running a marathon every second of every day, but it is not enough. At some point, you must DECIDE you are going to run a marathon and then go into strict training. The same is true with any goal or dream you desire to complete.

"Everyone who competes in the games goes into strict training. They do it to get a crown that will not last, but we do it to get a crown that will last forever." - 1 Corinthians 9:25 (NIV)

I believe in this scripture God is telling us that to fulfill our life's purpose, our goals and our dreams, we must go into strict training. No matter what we desire to do, we must go into strict training. There's only one little catch. To go into strict training, we must know what we are training for. If you are going to take a journey, you need to know where you're going. If you are going to run a race, you should know how far you intend to go for the best possible training.

I said earlier that you can successfully achieve your goals and dreams, but you must DECIDE what it is you want to accomplish. What is *your* goal? What do *you* want? How can you go into strict training for a race not knowing how many miles you will run? You can't. You would be running aimlessly with no purpose, direction, or plan. That's exactly what's happening to you if you have not decided what you want to do.

"I know your deeds, that you are neither cold nor hot. I wish you were either one or the other! So, because you are lukewarm—neither hot nor cold—I am about to spit you out of my mouth." - Revelation 3:15-16 (NIV)

God tells us our faith can be lukewarm, but I also believe we can be lukewarm when it comes to our goals, dreams, and, ultimately, our purpose. Lukewarm means you have one foot in and one foot out. If things are going in your favor and seem easy enough, you will try to accomplish things and think you are going to do it, but as soon as the first obstacle appears, or something doesn't go as planned, you give up and throw in the towel. I think the truth is that everyone wants to be successful. Ultimately, I wholeheartedly believe we are all born with a burning desire to achieve our purpose. God helps us understand our purpose through our dreams and the desires he places in our hearts. These desires are clues to our purpose. By using them, we can set goals.

The Bible teaches us that everyone is born with the innate understanding there is more to life than to live and die.

"For since the creation of the world God's invisible qualities—his eternal power and divine nature—have been clearly seen, being understood from what has been made, so that people are without excuse." - Romans 1:20 (NIV)

For as long as I can remember I have been going to church. I remember the church bus picking me up on Sunday mornings and carrying me off to Sunday school. I loved it. We would sing and read child appropriate Bible stories. I have very fond memories of church as a child. When I was 14, I accepted Christ as my Savior and was baptized. My intentions were good. I wanted to follow Christ, and I wanted to go to heaven. I wanted it so bad that I was good for a while. There was only one little issue. I wanted it, but I hadn't fully decided that the Christian life was how I was going to live. The problem was my mindset. I wanted it so bad, but I was lukewarm. I had one foot in heaven and one foot out in the world. If I was hanging around my church family, it was easy to be a Christian, but if I was with my worldly friends, then you can imagine what happened. My desire was to follow Christ, but my mindset was undecided. I wanted the best of both worlds. I was wandering aimlessly, and based on my experience, that did not turn out well.

If you are lukewarm with what it is you want to do, like I was as an early Christian wandering aimlessly back and forth, you most likely will not achieve success either.

A lukewarm mindset can be defined as an "I'll try" mindset. Both are predecessors to failure. Let me explain. Remember my friend Mary? When we started our first day of training for the two-mile run, I had an "I'll Try" mindset or attitude. I wanted to run, and it sounded like a great way to get myself in shape after having my youngest daughter, but I was lukewarm in my decision. On the other hand, Mary had already registered and paid money for the race. She had a decided mindset. Had it been left up to me, as soon as we realized we couldn't make it farther than fifty feet without gasping for air, the white flag would have been waved. Thankfully, Mary's decided mindset kept us going.

When we are lukewarm with an "I'll Try" mindset and wondering aimlessly, our decisions are made based on how we feel in the moment instead of making the more difficult choices necessary for us to ultimately be successful in whatever our goal is.

Can you picture an old movie with scenes from the pioneer days where the men would race to the property they wanted to have, stick a stake in the ground, and claim it for their own? This was how they could start a life for their family, and it must have been something to see. I don't remember the movie, but I remember seeing this man on a horse. He was carrying a great big stake with a flag on it, and he forced it into the ground he was claiming. It made my heart race watching him dash across the plains as fast as he could, most likely up against another settler trying to get there first. He was determined, and nothing was going to stop him from successfully claiming the property he desired.

Just like the settler in the pioneer days, you must lay claim on your goals and dreams. You must stick the stake in the ground and DECIDE this is what you are going to do. No matter what!

You must shift your mindset from an "I'll Try," lukewarm thought process to an "I've Decided" mindset. No matter what it is you desire to do, whatever your goals and dreams are, you must first DECIDE that you are going to do it. Pick up the stake and stick it in the ground. Lay claim on what belongs to you. There is no one else that can do what you were born to do. If you don't do it, then it will not happen. *Allow that to sink in.*

No matter what it is you want to achieve, it needs to follow the phrase "I've Decided to..."

I've Decided to lose weight. I've Decided to finish school. I've Decided to get out of debt. I've Decided to run my first 5K. I've Decided to get married. I've Decided to follow Jesus. I've Decided to open my own business. I've Decided to get organized. I've Decided to write a book. I've Decided to live natural. I've Decided to get married. I've Decided to buy a car. I've Decided to take a trip. I've Decided to change careers. I've Decided to be a better spouse or parent. I've Decided to homeschool. I've Decided to move. I've Decided to buy a house. I've Decided to have kids. I've Decided to be patient. I've Decided to be grateful. I've Decided to exercise. I've Decided to eat clean. I've Decided to learn more. I've Decided to trust. I've Decided to be a better friend. I've Decided to be happy. I've Decided to get up early. I've Decided to work less. I've Decided to spend more time with my family. I've Decided to volunteer and give back. I've Decided to journal or blog. I've Decided to live with purpose. I've Decided to quit smoking. I've Decided to get help. I've Decided to retire. I've Decided to save money. I've Decided to remodel my house. I've Decided to adopt or be a foster parent. I've Decided to be an encourager. I've Decided to be kind to others. I've Decided to stop speaking negatively. I've Decided to not curse. I've Decided to adopt a pet. I've Decided to live my life. I've Decided to go for the promotion. I've Decided to be positive. I've Decided to...

What is it that you want to do? What will you decide?

I've decided to...

_____

because I can!

You can decide to do whatever you want. So what is it? Take the first step and decide now to do it! Why? Because you can! Don't overthink it. Start small. Start with anything. I am going to teach you in this book how to apply the decide method to any goal you desire to achieve and be successful.

"I know your deeds, that you are neither cold nor hot. I wish you were either one or the other! So, because you are lukewarm—neither hot nor cold—I am about to spit you out of my mouth." - Revelation 3:15-16 (NIV)

Creating a shift in your mindset takes effort. It is an ongoing process which requires you to recommit to your goals daily. Although your goals may change, the process is the same. If you learn this process and put it into practice, you will be successful.

Have courage and fearlessly DECIDE to begin!

To be successful in whatever it is you have decided to do, you are going to have to be willing to make a change. There is nothing you can think of that wouldn't require some type of behavioral change. Turn back to the page where I have a list of goals to choose from. All of them would require you to make a change of some sort. From the smallest goal to the largest, you would need to change something to be successful. The main reason that most people are not successful in achieving their goals is because they refuse to make any necessary changes or believe the lie that they are incapable of the necessary change. They want the desired result, but without making the changes.

15

One small example of a change could be waking up early. How many times do you hear someone say, "I am not a morning person, and I can't wake up early." Maybe you've even said that yourself. If there is a goal you really want to achieve, it could possibly require you to wake up earlier to be successful. If you have the idea that you are not a morning person, and you refuse to change that behavior, then you could be missing out on a goal that is intended to move you closer to your life's purpose. You may desire the change but are unwilling to make it. Remember, insanity is doing the same thing over and over and expecting a different result. If you keep doing the same thing, you will continue to get the same results. To get a different outcome, something must change.

You can't keep doing what you've been doing and expect different results. Different results require different decisions, and different decisions require a different mindset!

When I decided to write this book, something had to change. I could not continue filling up all my time every day without allotting time to write. At some point, I had to sit at my computer, block other things out, and start typing. Otherwise, writing a book would still be on my list of goals. As I explained earlier in the book, I could want to run a marathon, just like I could want to write a book, but wanting something is not enough. In fact, wanting something breeds an "I'll Try" mindset. For fun, go back to the dream list and instead of putting the phrase "I've decided to...," say, "I'm going to try to..." It doesn't even sound right does it? The fact remains, until you DECIDE, you are simply lukewarm and wandering aimlessly. To be successful in our goals, we must go into strict training. No matter what you desire to do, strict training is an absolute must, just like the Apostle Paul reminds us.

"Everyone who competes in the games goes into strict training. They do it to get a crown that will not last, but we do it to get a crown that will last forever." - 1 Corinthians 9:25 (NIV)

You are ready to learn and apply the process if you have decided on your goal and are willing to make some necessary changes to be successful. What is it you want to accomplish? Until you can answer that, nothing can happen.

I've decided to...

_____

because I can!

To help make the learning process of changing a behavior and shifting your mindset from "I'll Try" to "I've Decided" a little easier, I have simplified the steps into an easy to use acrostic. Can you guess what it is? Yes, DECIDE! I have taken each letter in the word DECIDE and correlated it to the steps in the behavioral change process to make it easy for you to remember, learn, and apply to successfully complete your goals and dreams.

DECIDE is a six-step behavioral change methodology that I believe works, and it is simple enough for anyone to follow.

The six steps are:

- **D**eclare
- **E**nvision
- **C**ultivate
- **I**ncorporate
- **D**evelop Discipline
- **E**xcel

Remember, achieving your goal is like running a marathon. Every step forward gets you closer to the finish line!

2. DECLARE

The first step in shifting your mindset and successfully achieving whatever it is that you've decided to do is to **Declare**. What does it mean to declare? The word "declare" means to say something in a solemn and empathetic manner or to take possession of. When you declare something solemnly, you are, in other words, taking possession of it. "I am declaring that I am going to achieve this goal, and it belongs to me!" Remember, you were born to do things that no one else can do. To declare also means to make known publicly or to someone. You must verbally declare what your intentions are. The first person you need to declare to is yourself! You should speak out loud what you are going to do. You must get the goal from your mind to your mouth and verbalize it out loud. Let's practice. Say aloud what it is you have decided to do.

I've decided to…

_____

because I can!

Declare this out loud too. "I believe that God has put this desire in my heart, and He wants me to be successful!"

You must declare the truth!

Yes, God desires for you to achieve success in your goals and dreams. In fact, He has already paved the way.

"What, then, shall we say in response to these things? If God is for us, who can be against us?" - Romans 8:31 (NIV)

"So do not fear, for I am with you; do not be dismayed, for I am your God. I will strengthen you and help you; I will uphold you with my righteous right hand." - Isaiah 41:10 NIV

God is holding YOU in His right hand. Let that sink in.

What is it you want to accomplish? Do not keep it tucked away as your own little secret. Remember, to declare means to make public. You need to make your goals known. Not everyone needs to know, so be selective with whom you share your intentions. You may want to ask yourself a few leading questions: Who could you share your goals with that would encourage you and be a supporter? Who is someone who would hold you accountable and not allow you to wave the white flag easily or throw in the towel? Who loves you enough to be honest with you but would not be too much of a devil's advocate? There isn't a magic number on how many people you make your goals known to. It really depends on what you are planning to do and the importance you place on your goal.

Earlier in the first chapter I shared with you my story about growing up in a church and my fond memories. I accepted Jesus as my savior at the age of 14 and was baptized. Although I wanted to follow Jesus and my intentions were good, my heart was only half in. I wanted the best of both worlds. I desired to go to heaven, but I wanted to live the fun teenage life, too, doing what my worldly friends were doing. I was a lukewarm Christian, and it did not turn out well for me. I eventually stopped going to church, and my worldly desires took over. I believe there are a few reasons this happened. One, I had an "I'll Try" mindset instead of a decided one. I wanted to live a godly life, but I never fully declared it solemnly or took possession of it. Two, I never told anyone who could hold me accountable, support and encourage me, or who loved me enough to not let me throw in the towel on my decision. My goal was to follow Jesus and live a godly life, but because I never stuck the stake in the ground and decided this was what I was going to do, nor did I take the first step in my behavioral change by declaring my goal to a few important people, I was not successful. I could also add I wasn't willing to make the changes necessary for success. Remember, to be successful in your goals, you must be willing to make some changes. You must *declare* that you need to change.

One of my favorite pictures was taken when I finally made the decision to take possession of my goal, and I fully decided to follow Jesus. I stuck the stake in the ground and claimed ownership. I love to show this picture in my live presentations when I am teaching on "declare," the first step in the DECIDE method. It is a picture of my second baptism as an adult and was taken about four years ago. In the picture, I am coming up out of the water with my hands held high by two pastors of the church I attended, and it was in front of at least fifty other church members. This was a very important goal for me, and I wanted to make my decision public. You can imagine the accountability I have, the support and encouragement. I wouldn't always suggest declaring on such a public basis, but in this situation, it was fitting. It is the best visual of declaration I have.

You must get the goal from your mind to your mouth!

When I was coaching one of my clients who wanted to lose weight, I was hoping to help her understand her "why" for her weight loss goal, and so I asked her these two questions: What is it you want to do, and when you think about your future, what do you want it to look like? Her answer surprised me. She said, "I want to buy an RV and travel back and forth to my kids' homes and spend time with them and my grandchildren." The tears welled up in her eyes. I believe she got so emotional because, for the first time, she spoke what her real goal was. She got the goal from her mind to her mouth and professed it to me, a real person! Yes, she wanted to lose weight, but that was just the first step toward achieving her actual long-term desire.

Hopefully you are feeling confident that you need to declare your goals. If you are going to be successful in achieving your goal, then you will need to take the first step in the DECIDE method and declare. Who will you declare to? Make a list of people with whom you would consider sharing your intentions, dreams, and goals.

Who could you share your goals with that would encourage you and be a supporter?

1. _____
2. _____
3. _____

Who is someone who would hold you accountable and not allow you to wave the white flag easily or throw in the towel?

1. _____
2. _____
3. _____

Who loves you enough to be honest with you but would not be too much of a devil's advocate?

1. _____
2. _____
3. _____

There is no magic number on who or how many people to tell. But, you must declare to someone who will hold you accountable, and of course, always start by declaring to yourself first!

From that moment on, you must immediately begin to envision what will happen if you achieve or don't achieve your goals.

3. ENVISION

The next step is the **E** in **DECIDE,** and it is to Envision.

I love the word envision. The definition literally means to conceive as a possibility or to mentally picture a future event. From the moment you make the declaration of your goal, you must immediately start to visualize each step you will take along the journey and what the result or your destination will be. You must conceive it as a possibility.

When I started my running journey, it was a pitiful beginning. I would head out and barely make it to the next mailbox without gasping for air. I could have easily given up, and I wanted to. Remember that I had an accountability partner named Mary? She was already decided, and that encouraged me to be decided. So, I kept going. Every day as I would head out to run, I would imagine myself going just a little farther than the day before. You know what? Most days I could go a little farther. My initial goal in running was to go a little farther than the day before. I started to dream about the race day for the two-mile run. How I would feel, what I would wear, and about all the people who would be watching. I visualized every step of the race in my mind over and over. I even lost some weight, so I started thinking about wearing cute shorts and running clothes. I could literally feel the emotions, and I would just keep focused on that. We trained for the two months leading up to the race, and all the while I was envisioning the entire event.

I tell everyone I coach in living a healthy lifestyle they must start envisioning the process of losing weight immediately. I let them know that they should start seeing themselves how they want to be, picturing the healthy choices they are now making. I say to them, "Visualize yourself exercising every day and making healthy meal options. Focus on who you are becoming, how you will feel, what you will look like, the newfound energy, and no medications or health issues because of unhealthy choices."

Whatever your goal is, you must conceive it as a possibility and act as though you are already successful.

Keep your eye on the prize!

What is your goal?

I've decided to...

_____

                                  because I can!

You should envision yourself successfully completing this goal constantly. Imagine your life once you have accomplished it. Focus on the positive impact it will have on you and those you love.

A great way to envision is to create vision boards. You can place pictures of what you want and pictures that represent your future self. I like to use pictures that represent the positive changes which will occur if I accomplish my goal.

The word envision means to mentally picture a future event. The reality is that future events are usually the consequences of the choices we make today.

What I choose today will determine my tomorrow!

Focusing on all the positive changes that would occur if you successfully complete your goal is a great way to stay on track and keep yourself looking on the bright side. Unfortunately, there is an alternative outcome. You should have the tough conversation with yourself and ask, "What if I don't achieve success?" A future will still exist even if you don't achieve success.

Of course, there are a lot of goals you could have that most likely would not be detrimental to your future to an extreme. Maybe you would like to travel somewhere you've never been or remodel your house. You may like the thought of a job promotion or finishing school, but you could survive living on the salary you have now. These are all amazing goals, but not necessarily detrimental if you don't accomplish them. However, I would advise that you should still envision yourself being successful or not successful in every goal. Imagine what the future would be like with both outcomes.

When I was in my late teens and twenties, I had the terrible habit of smoking. I knew it was a bad addiction, and I had seen the results of it in my family. My grandpa died of emphysema. I wanted to quit and spent almost every day thinking of ways to help myself kick the habit. I hated being a smoker, and I didn't want the consequences of smoking for my future self.

I spent a lot of time envisioning myself as a nonsmoker. I imagined not feeling the overwhelming desire to smoke and the money I would save. I visualized my future self being healthy, happy, and free from any diseases brought on by smoking. These were all great things, and the most likely consequences if I completed my goal of quitting smoking.

I spent most of my twenties smoking on and off between bouts of quitting and then giving in to the temptation when I would come up against an obstacle like stress or being around others smoking. I could never totally kick the habit. I did quit for a few years while having my daughters, but I eventually started smoking on the rare occasion when they were very young.

Again, I started the process of quitting and going through the on-and-off-again phase. I hated it, and I didn't like myself much for being held captive to this addiction.

I remember the first time I started envisioning my future self if I didn't complete my goal of quitting smoking. I met a lady who became a dear friend of mine. She was and still is beautiful inside and out. Unfortunately, she is facing the consequences of years of smoking, and I am a witness to her symptoms. It makes me so sad to see this beautiful person, healthy otherwise, unable to walk far without breathing problems. I remember thinking, *Lord please help me. I don't want to end up in this same situation.* From that point on, I started envisioning my future self being unsuccessful. I thought about how most people didn't even know I smoked and would be shocked when they realized I did. I would see myself carrying around an oxygen tank and unable to play with my future grandchildren. I would picture my kids standing around a hospital bed shaking their heads in disbelief, and I remember even imagining being told I had cancer and was going to die. Granted, these are extreme visions, but they worked! When I would get to a point where I felt the addiction starting to take over my will power, I would begin to think on these negative outcomes. I would experience a surge of discipline that would get me through the urge to smoke.

I continued to envision all the positive outcomes of quitting and seeing myself totally free of the addiction, but at times when I felt weak and wanted to give in and smoke a cigarette, I would kick it up a notch and envision the future with the consequences that would come about if I gave in to the temptation. Envisioning the future picture with the positive and negative outcomes worked for me. I decided to quit smoking!

I have seen this step work for my clients who want to lose weight. I have them envision themselves sick and unhealthy as an overweight future self when they feel the urge to throw in the towel. Of course, you always continue to think of the positive outcome, but somehow the negative consequence can really keep you motivated during the trying times.

Envision is the E in DECIDE and the second step in successfully completing your goal.

"Our imagination is God's ingenious gift that hands us the privilege of romping and playing in realities that we can't see only because we've yet to create them." - Craig D. Lounsbrough

I've decided to...

_____
                              because I can!

Take this space to write down or draw some pictures of the positive outcomes you can envision that will be in your future if you are successful, as well as what the outcomes would be if you don't successfully complete your goals.

Either option will have a future.

4. CULTIVATE

The **C** in DECIDE stands for **Cultivate.** The third step in shifting from an "I'll Try" mindset to an "I've Decided" mindset so that you can successfully complete your goals is to cultivate. This term means to acquire or develop. The word cultivate is an action word. The idea is that what action you take will ultimately determine how you think and how you feel. If you wait until the moment when all the stars are aligned and you literally "feel" like taking the first step, it most likely will never happen. Although it's true you could muster up the energy at some point to get yourself started, that energy will quickly begin to subside and the "feeling" will no longer match the actions you need to take.

You must acquire and develop the mindset of the emotion which follows the action. It is rarely ever the other way around. When you cultivate this attitude on a continual basis, your life will change.

I have been running for twelve years. To this day, I still hit the snooze button when my alarm goes off in the morning. I don't "feel" like getting out of my warm, cozy bed. However, once I get up, my feet hit the pavement, and I have finished my run, the emotion follows. I have never regretted a run once I have completed it!

Take captive each thought and align it to your goals. People who live decided do not make decisions based on how they feel. They make decisions based on what their goals are.

The emotion will follow the action.

Romans 12:12 (NIV) reminds us to be transformed by the renewing of our mind so that we can test and approve what God's good, pleasing, and perfect will is.

The word "acquire" means to learn or develop a skill, habit, or quality. As you start to cultivate this mindset you will see new patterns of thinking begin to take shape. It takes practice, and you will need to take captive every thought and align it to your new way of thinking. For a while, it will not come naturally, and the old ways of not "feeling" like it will creep in, but when you're intentional about your thoughts, and what you do with them, you can change!

"We demolish arguments and every pretension that sets itself up against the knowledge of God, and we take captive every thought to make it obedient to Christ." - 2 Corinthians 10:5 (NIV)

When you experience the transformation in your life that occurs when your daily actions (decisions) match the desires, dreams, and goals you have deep within you, and you don't allow your emotions to determine your actions (decisions), nothing you set in front of you will be impossible.

When I first started running, it was the most difficult thing I had ever done. It was painful, I would get winded almost immediately as soon as I started running, and I would literally gasp for air. My muscles were sore, and I felt like I could never be a runner. If I had made my decisions based off these feelings, I would have missed out on all the benefits from running over the years. Instead, I cultivated the mindset that although I didn't "feel" like working hard, nor did I "feel" like going into strict training, it would get easier if I would just keep at it. Guess what? It did!

What is it that you want to do? What is your goal?

I've decided to…

_____

because I can!

Take captive every thought that doesn't align with your goal and make it obedient to God's perfect will for you. It takes practice and constant effort, but you can do it! Remember the emotion will follow the action.

"I can do all this through Him who gives me strength."
Philippians 4:13 NIV

It is important to be completely aware of your thoughts and how you are making your decisions if you are going to successfully complete your goal. **Cultivate** is to acquire and develop!

Take the next section to write down some thoughts you need to take captive that don't match your goals and are based on feelings.

These thoughts could start with: I don't feel like it, or I'm just too tired. You may say something like, "I should have started years ago. It's too late now." If your goal is an emotional change, such as "I've decided to be patient," You may have believed a lie that you are just an impatient person and that's just the way you are. That is not true! Patience is a behavior, and behaviors can be learned and changed.

What are some thoughts you need to take captive and align to your goal?

You are absorbing a ton of information, and at this point, you may be pondering if there is a shortcut to all of this. I am sorry to say I have never met anyone who has successfully achieved their goals by taking the easy way out or a shortcut. Behavioral change takes much effort and a determination like no other. Changing your mindset from an "I'll Try" to an "I've Decided" mindset requires you to be patient. Go easy on yourself when you make mistakes.

I love to say, **"Don't be afraid to make mistakes. Know that you will, and go for it anyway!"**

The truth is, no matter what it is you are trying to do, you will make a mistake. Mistakes are simply that, mistakes. God's grace is new every day, so you can pick up right where you left off. I assure you there is no one who has ever went into strict training that didn't make a mistake.

Yes, when you make a mistake, you will "feel" disappointed, and maybe you will "feel" like you can't do it, but remember, as a decided person, you no longer make decisions based on how you feel. You make decisions based on your goals. This is the mindset you are cultivating. Look at it this way. Disappointment is not disaster. Although you feel disappointed, and you should, when you make a decision that doesn't align with your goals, it doesn't determine the outcome. What you do with the disappointment is more important. If I had thrown in the towel every time I made a mistake and smoked a cigarette or took a drag while I was quitting, I would still be a smoker. No, when I made that mistake, I recommitted to my goal and kept on going. This is what you must do as well.

A mistake is a disappointment, and a disappointment is not a disaster. Throwing in the towel and quitting on your goal, now *that* is disaster!

Cultivate a different mindset so that you will successfully achieve your goals!

***

How are you doing so far? Thinking of the effort it is going to take for you to achieve success can be exhausting.

This is a great time to lay your book down for a moment and mediate on God's word, pray over your goals, relax, and rest in Him.

"but those who hope in the Lord will renew their strength. They will soar on wings like eagles; they will run and not grow weary, they will walk and not be faint." - Isaiah 40:31 (NIV)

Meditate on that scripture for a while and let it sink in.

NOTES:

5. INCORPORATE

The **I** in DECIDE is **incorporate.** The fourth step in changing your mindset from "I'll Try" to an "I've Decided" mindset and successfully achieving your goals is to incorporate.

Incorporate means to unite or work into something already in existence to form an indistinguishable whole or to blend and combine thoroughly. In other words, you and your goal already exist. You just need to blend in and combine some outside sources and your own internal reasoning behind why you want to achieve your goals to become whole, which will ultimately lead to success.

The first thing you need to incorporate is your "why." Your "why" is your X-factor, and your X-factor is the variable in any given situation that could have the most significant impact on your outcome. What is the reason you want to accomplish your goal? For example, if I want to lose weight, I could simply say I just want to look good and feel good. Yes, and so does the rest of the world, but why do I want to look better and feel better? You should keep asking yourself leading questions until you get to the truth behind why you really want to achieve your goal. What is your burning desire for the ultimate result to be? What will be different in your life if you complete your goal?

Here are a couple of examples.

Why did I begin the organization I've Decided? Because I have a burning desire to motivate and encourage others to be successful, which I believe, in turn, will bring about my own success. Additionally, I desire to be a legacy woman. I want to leave an inheritance for my children's children. I want to know at the end of my life that I made a difference which will last long after I'm gone from this earth. I expect to meet my heavenly Father, and I want to hear Him say, "Well done my good and faithful servant." That is the ultimate result for me and my life's goal.

Remember the lady I was coaching who shared her ultimate reason with me as to why she wanted to lose weight? She wanted to buy an RV and travel back and forth between her children's homes and spend time and play with her grandchildren. She could have easily said she just wanted to look better and feel better, but that would not have been the variable that had the most impact on her outcome. "I want to lose weight to look better and feel better" is not a tangible reason. How I feel about my looks, and ultimately how I feel about my energy, could change daily. It is not something I can easily incorporate into myself and my goals that already exist. However, owning an RV, driving across country between my children's homes, and playing outside with my grandchildren are all things that I can envision. Remember Step 2 of changing your mindset from an "I'll Try" to an "I've Decided" mindset requires you to envision your future. Your "why" behind your goal, or your X-factor, must be tangible. It should be something you can envision and incorporate into your mindset when the obstacles show up.

Oh, and the obstacles will show up!

Be alert and of sober mind. Your enemy the devil prowls around like a roaring lion looking for someone to devour.
- 1 Peter 5:8 (NIV)

In Ephesians 6:16, the Word refers to the devil's evil schemes as fiery arrows. The point is that the devil hates you, and he is your enemy. The devil does not want you to successfully fulfill your goals and dreams. So, what does he do? He prowls around looking for an opportune time to devour you or throw a fiery arrow at you. A lot of times these fiery arrows show up in the form of obstacles. I like to call them daggers. This is the devil's evil scheme to knock us down and keep us from success. You, like many others, may believe that it is the devil's job to tempt us to sin. Have you ever heard the phrase, "The devil made me do it"? I believe this is the devil's biggest lie he pulls off. If our enemy can get us to believe that his only job is to cause us to sin, then he can pull the wool over our eyes and catch us off guard. The truth is that Jesus died for our sin. If you believe that and you have placed your trust and faith in what God did on that cross, as well as raising Jesus from the dead, then you are dead to sin and alive in Christ. Sin no longer has dominion over you.

"For sin shall no longer be your master, because you are not under the law, but under grace." - Romans 6:14 NIV

Sin is not the devil's concern. The enemy's concern is keeping you from fulfilling your God-given purpose. The devil's job is to do everything he can to prevent you from fulfilling your goals and dreams. Do not forget that you have an enemy who hates you and does not want you to be successful. It will get him angry when you stick the stake in the ground and start to learn this process of living with an "I've Decided" mindset. You can be prepared for these daggers by always putting on your spiritual armor as Ephesians 6 teaches us. You can also be ready to fire back with your "why" that you have incorporated into your mindset. If you are clear on your X-factor and have been honest with your reason behind achieving your goals, then you can constantly remind yourself about the importance of you why you need to achieve success. This is incorporating your "why" or your variable that will have the most influence on your outcome.

To incorporate the "why" behind your goal is your personal motivation behind your decision to DECIDE in the first place. I will be honest. This is probably the hardest part of shifting your mindset from "I'll Try" to "I've Decided." It is, however, the most important. It requires some deep thinking and soul searching. Getting to the root, or the heart, of the matter can be emotional and sometimes painful. Often, we have a hard time verbalizing what our "why" is because we are concerned about what others will think. For years, I never admitted I had a goal to be a motivational speaker. I was embarrassed, and I believed people would think I was arrogant or boastful if I said that I felt called to be a motivational speaker. I imagined them saying negative and hurtful things behind my back such as, "Who does she think she is?" or "I can't believe she wants to be a motivational speaker." I allowed what others thought to hold me back from my goal and, ultimately, my God-given purpose. Do not concern yourself with what others will say in regards to your goals and your "why" behind them.

You have to be willing to feel a little uncomfortable, dig deep, and pray for God's help in determining the "why" behind your goal or X-factor.

I've decided to...

_____

because I can!

What is the reason you are wanting to successfully complete this goal? What variable has the most significant impact on your outcome?

What is your why?

_____

_____

_____

_____

_____

_____

_____

_____

_____

_____

_____

_____

_____

You will also need to incorporate the right people of influence who will have the capacity to affect your character and the development of your behavior in a positive way.

Be careful the environment you choose for it will shape you; be careful the friends you choose for you will become like them. ~ W. Clement Stone

Think back to earlier in the book when I was sharing about my friend, Mary, who had asked me to run a two-mile fun run with her. My first time out to run was a disaster. I made it fifty feet, was gasping for air, and every cell of my body was hurting. I was ready to throw in the towel on running after the first time out. I had an "I'll Try" mindset, but, thankfully, Mary had an "I've Decided" mindset. Mary had already registered for the race and had stuck the stake in the ground to claim what belonged to her. Because Mary was a huge influence on my training, and she was decided, we kept up the training. Twelve years later, I am still a runner.

This is just one example, and I believe it is proof that the people you're surrounding yourself with will influence your decision making and mindset. You must incorporate the right influences or, in other words, the right accountability partners. I like to call them accountabilibuddies!

The best way to ensure you are successful in achieving your goal is to find someone who has already accomplished what you have decided to do. Statistically, you become like the five people you most hang around. That is a very interesting statistic, but I think it could be somewhat inaccurate.

A few years ago, I wanted to run a half marathon in under

two hours. It was a goal I had wanted to accomplish for a while. I had been running along at the same pace for many years, and I was ready to step it up a notch. I had a running buddy and dear friend with whom I ran four out of my five marathons, but due to work schedules, we were rarely running together much anymore. I knew if I was going to accomplish my goal of running a half marathon in under two hours, I would need to find an accountabilibuddy to keep me on track and push me to work harder than I had been.

I needed to incorporate an outside source to blend in to my already existent goal. The perfect person was the mom of one of my daughter's friends at school. We had talked many times, and I knew she was a little faster runner than me from races past. One day after school, I talked to her about running and asked if I could join her sometime. She said yes! There was a slight stipulation. She ran in the morning, beginning between 4:30 and 5:00 a.m.! Holy earliness, Batman! Remember, to be successful in achieving your goal, you must be willing to make some changes. I decided that this would work, and we went into strict training. It was hard waking up, it was hard keeping up, and it was hard in general, but it was necessary if I was going to beat my time goal. I am happy to report I successfully ran the Susan G. Komen half marathon in October of 2014 in under two hours. (On a side note, I am still running early with my dear friend who has now become one of my best friends.) You never know what will happen when you successfully achieve a goal or where it will take you.

Only God knows.

"For I know the plans I have for you," declares the LORD, "plans to prosper you and not to harm you, plans to give you hope and a future." - Jerimiah 29:11 (NIV)

Who is your accountabilibuddy?

_____

Who are the people of influence that you will incorporate into your life and goal?

1. _____
2. _____
3. _____
4. _____
5. _____

You may want to consider incorporating a mentor, as well. This is a person that has most likely accomplished what you have set as a goal or something similar. Their story should inspire you, and their character should be one you aspire to be like. Your mentor should be willing to give you honest advice, and someone who cares about your successful outcome. They will push you beyond your comfort zone while keeping you realistic. If you have someone in mind, it is perfectly okay for you to ask them to be your mentor.

To achieve success in your goal, you will need to incorporate resources. Resources can be services or other assets that will meet your needs which will arise while working toward your goal. If your goal is to run, then you would need good shoes and some running gear. Maybe you want to get out of debt, then you could use some help with a budget. If your goal is to get healthy, then you will need a coach and some nutritional guidance. Whatever it is that you have decided to do, you will need the right resources to be successful.

Personal development, educational seminars, businesses which provide a product or service you need, and other people in general who are working toward their goals for inspiration would all be considered resources or assets.

Take a moment and think about the resources or assets you will need to successfully achieve your goal and write them below.

- _____
- _____
- _____
- _____
- _____
- _____

To recap, the I in DECIDE and the fourth step to shifting from an "I'll Try" mindset to an "I've Decided" mindset so that you will be successful in your goals is to incorporate your "why" or X-factor, the right people of influence, and the resources and assets you will need.

Incorporate!

6. DEVELOP DISCIPLINE

The **D** in DECIDE is to **Develop Discipline.** The fifth step in changing your mindset from an "I'll Try" to an "I've Decided" mindset is to develop discipline.

Let's start with the word develop. "Develop" means to grow or change into a more advanced, larger, or stronger form. I love the word develop because it encourages me to know that I can develop anything I DECIDE to develop. I can develop a positive, loving, and grateful attitude, a different mindset, better relationships, a healthy lifestyle, a fitter body, patience, and so much more! I just need to remember that the word change is included in the definition! In order to develop something into a more advanced, larger, or stronger form, something else must change, and that's the hard part. A lot of times, we are comfortable right where we are or so set in our ways that we are not willing to make the necessary changes.

Science teaches us that we have developed a certain pattern of thinking and behaviors from the time we are born. These behaviors come from natural personality tendencies as well as outside influences like out parents, immediate family members, and surroundings. From the moment we are born, these influences start making a way into our minds, and we form behaviors based off of them. These behaviors start to become as natural to us as breathing. They are so close to us that we can't notice any behaviors that could be harming us or holding us back from being the best we can be. Of course, we all have some good behaviors, but on the flip side, we all have some bad behaviors, too.

The good news is that behaviors (habits) can change!

As an example, a person can be born predominantly right handed. They can write and work with their right hand most of their life, and it is all they know. If they try to do anything left handed, it feels uncomfortable, and so they never attempt to use their left side most of the time. All of us can understand this analogy because you were either born right handed or left handed (very few can use both,) and it feels weird using your non-dominant hand.

Now, let's take a person who has been injured somehow. Maybe they've had a stroke, and the stroke caused them to be paralyzed on their dominant side. Think about what happens. They begin therapy using their less dominant side, and they are forced into a situation where they must use the arm in which they haven't used until now. Of course, it feels awkward and strange at first, but because they have no other option, they continue practicing, working, and pushing through any uncomfortable feelings that occur. Essentially, they go into strict training. Why? Because they know if they don't figure out how to use the non-dominant side, they will be held back from basic tasks like eating, dressing, combing their hair, and brushing their teeth. They develop their non-dominant side and, eventually, it becomes more advanced and stronger. People who are born without arms or legs go into strict training, as well. They learn un-instinctual ways to get things done, like driving a car with their feet instead of arms or brushing their teeth and eating with their toes instead of fingers. We've all seen miraculous stories of people who do seemingly impossible tasks because they decided they were not going to sit around and feel sorry for themselves.

My friend Derrick Tennant can tie his shoe with one hand because his left side is paralyzed. These stories are amazing, but they are also proof that, given the right motivation and situation, behaviors and mindsets (even those we're born with) can be changed.

If a person can teach themselves how to use their non-dominant side under distressed circumstances, then you most certainly can achieve your goal. You simply need to believe you can change and understand how to know it's possible.

You must believe you can change and have an "I've Decided" mindset!

The fifth step to change from an "I'll Try" to and "I've Decided" mindset is to develop discipline.

How do I know for certain that you can change your behaviors? Science proves it, and it's called neuroplasticity.

Neuroplasticity is the brain's ability to reorganize itself by forming new neural connections throughout life. Neuroplasticity backs up the biblical scripture found in Romans 12:2 (NIV) that states we should be transformed by the renewing of our mind. We can renew (change) our mind (behaviors).

Neuroplasticity is why people who are born with physical disabilities, such as missing a limb or have been paralyzed, can learn a new way of doing whatever it is they desire to do. Their brain reorganizes itself to create or change an already existing behavior.

Imagine these patterns in your brain (behaviors) that happen automatically because it's the way you've always thought or done something. Over and over you take the same pattern until eventually there is a groove. The groove that has been formed is now the easiest path of resistance. So, naturally, it's the path you will take. To change this path of least resistance, you will need to build a new groove. This will take work, but you can do it! Most people wait until they've hit rock bottom to start to create a new groove, but you don't have to do that. You can begin now by developing a new mindset.

Maybe you've heard of the snowball analogy. It is a great way to understand neuroplasticity. Believe it or not, everyone has a different reaction to a snowball being thrown at them. When you were a kid, maybe you grew up in an area that had no snow so you never experienced having a snowball thrown at you. This could spark a different reaction then someone who grew up in a snowy area with lots of siblings who played daily with snow and had a tremendous amount of fun having friendly snowball fights with their brothers, sisters, and friends. However, what about the kid who was picked on constantly by an older brother or a neighborhood bully that would throw snowballs in a mean and harmful way? You can imagine that their reaction to a snowball being thrown at them would be much different. If I throw a snowball at someone whose brain goes down the memory groove of how much fun snow is, they will most likely pick up snow, laugh, and start a friendly snowball fight. On the flipside, if I throw a snowball and it hits the back of someone's head whose thoughts go down the memory groove of the bully who used to try and hurt them with snowballs, the scene is going to be much different. This is one example of neuroplasticity.

I know you can be successful in your goal and change your mindset because I have been successful in achieving my goals and changing certain behaviors. I went from being a couch potato and overweight to a healthy weight and running five marathons. I've kicked bad habits such as smoking, cursing, and road rage. You can do it too!

I have a robust personality. I can be loud, stubborn, and sometimes act on the aggressive side. These are some natural tendencies I was either born with or had instilled in me so early in life that I can't remember not having them. I am also the youngest in my family and tend to want what I want now with very little patience. Most of my life, I have been labeled as an impatient person, and I even labeled myself as impatient. So, guess how I behaved? Yes, impatient! As you can imagine, my impatient behavioral pattern has caused me much grief over my life, and it is what the Lord started working on in my heart very shortly after my baptism as an adult.

He started to gently nudge me while driving in my car. I would get so mad if I got stopped at a red light while in a hurry. Ridiculous, I know, but true. If someone pulled out in front of me, waited too long to go at a stoplight, or was driving in front of me slower than I thought they should, it was all over. I would lose my joy, get annoyed, and be ready to fight all in about twenty seconds flat. This is called road rage. I had terrible road rage, and the Lord intended for me to change that behavior. I started hearing this still small voice every time I would get worked up while in the car driving that would say, "That's not who you are." My first thought was,

"Yes, it is. I am impatient." I would hear it again. "No, you are my child now, and you should not behave in this manner."

It put the desire in my heart to want to change.

"Take delight in the Lord, and he will give you the desires of your heart." - Psalm 37:4 (NIV)

This went on for a while, and of course I continued to get road rage. At this point, I only *wanted* to change. I hadn't *decided* to change. I had an "I'll Try" mindset instead of an "I've Decided" mindset. I continued to hear the Lord's still small voice every time I would get mad. I am not kidding you. I could leave work in the best mood and full of joy, only to get barely out of the parking lot before some unknown person in an unknown car had ruined my entire mood by not driving the way I thought they should. God continued to nudge me, and the nudges became stronger, ever so gently.

Once, I was teaching a class to my Curves members on the DECIDE method and the six steps it takes to successfully achieve your goals and change behaviors, and would you believe it dawned on me? Maybe, I thought, I should utilize what I teach to help me overcome this ridiculous road rage. Ha! Now that's a thought. I took the first step that day and declared to my members that I was going to overcome road rage. From there, I started the process of creating a new groove in my mind for my thoughts to go down. I began envisioning myself being patient while in the car, relaxed, and not in a rush to get where I needed to be. I envisioned God smiling proudly down on me while I practiced acting like His child instead of a heathen. On the chance I didn't successfully overcome my road rage, I would envision rear ending someone and getting a reckless driving ticket or, worse, hurting someone because of my inexcusable anger. I cultivated the mindset that the emotion follows the action, and when I would make a mistake and get mad, I would start all over. I incorporated resources like listening to religious talk radio on a regular basis, and when my mind started to go down the old groove of road rage with negative talk, I took captive that thought and aligned it with the truth. What is the truth? The truth is that patience is not a character issue but a behavioral issue. It is a learned behavior that I had trained my mindset to be like.

My impatient groove (neuroplasticity) was deeper than my patient groove, and so being impatient, which caused my road rage, was the path of least resistance. I needed to develop my patience, which meant I needed to go into strict training to develop discipline.

Discipline is defined as training expected to produce a specific character or pattern of behavior, especially training that produces moral or mental improvement. Discipline is what is required for you to build a new groove for the changes you need to make. Since, naturally, your mind wants to go down the path of least resistance, you must be intentional about the choice you are going to make and how you are going to react. When someone reacts without giving much thought or based on how they feel at that time, they are most likely not practicing discipline. Discipline requires practice. When you are practicing discipline, you are almost always going against what you desire right at that moment. For example, when someone would sit at a green light in front of me longer than I thought they should, what I wanted to do at that moment was lay on my horn and let them know how annoyed I was at them. The desire to be impatient at that time was my deepest groove, the one which was the path of least resistance. To put discipline into practice, I had to intentionally take my annoyance and talk myself off the ledge.

I would say something like, "Kim, you are not in that much of a hurry, so don't get upset." Or, "Lord, you must want me to be here longer to avoid an accident down the road." I would crank my worship music, sing, and praise God. Doing this was going against the grain, and I had to make myself practice patience. Eventually, in time, my patient groove while in the car became deeper than my road rage groove, and thus became the path of least resistance. I overcame the bad behavior of road rage and achieved my goal.

Another example could be when someone has decided to lose weight. They may have a behavior of eating cereal each night before bed, and this is something they have decided to stop doing to make losing weight a little easier. Their behavioral groove of eating cereal in the beginning is much deeper than their behavioral groove of not eating the cereal. To overcome this bad behavior, they must practice discipline, which starts to create a new groove. In time, that groove will become the deepest and then be the path of least resistance.

Developing discipline takes time and lots of practice. Consider discipline a mental muscle. When you are trying to build strong muscles, you must put more resistance on the muscles than they are used to for those muscles to get stronger. The same is true for your mental muscle, discipline. If you use weights to build stronger body muscles, then think of practice as your weight to build stronger discipline, your mental muscle. The more you practice, the stronger your discipline will become. You must practice!

I started out practicing discipline to help overcome the bad behavior of road rage, but in doing so, my patience has filtered into other areas of my life. In fact, I no longer label myself as impatient. I grab hold of any thought that comes in my mind regarding my being impatient, and I align it to truth. The truth is that I am a child of the Highest King, and I can be patient. When I make a mistake, I recognize that it is not a disaster. It is a disappointment. I start over and keep practicing. The more I practice, the stronger my discipline becomes. The more areas of your life that you practice discipline in, the more disciplined you will be all around.

People who live with an "I've Decided" mindset must live with discipline, which can be described as making a choice right now that aligns with your long-term goals. People who live with an "I'll Try" mindset make choices based on their emotions and how they feel at the moment. This is called being reactive. When your day-to-day choices do not align with your long-term goal, it will be virtually impossible to experience success on any level.

While practicing discipline, just like in cultivating a mindset of the emotion following the action, you will make mistakes. At some point, you will make a choice that doesn't align with your goal or dream. When this happens, it is critical for you to forgive yourself and recognize the disappointment. It is not the end of the world. It does not give you permission or an easy way out to throw in the towel on your goal. It simply means you momentarily forgot what you had decided to do.

Even still, every now and then, I will forget that I no longer get road rage and start to get frustrated while behind someone driving slow. It doesn't mean that I am incapable of being patient or have not achieved my goal. It just means I made a mistake. For a brief moment, I forgot the decision I made. My old behavior was trying to creep back in and my brain was trying to go down the old groove. This is normal.

The same is true in living as child of God. Most days, I walk in who I am and behave as such. But, on some days when my emotions are flying high because of life's stresses at work or at home, I forget who I am. When this happens, I may act out of character and behave more like a devil child instead of God's child. But, I am quickly able to remember who I am and get my actions back in align with my goal of living as a child of God. The more I practice discipline, the easier it becomes, and it will be the same for you too.

"No discipline seems pleasant at the time, but painful. Later on, however, it produces a harvest of righteousness and peace for those who have been trained by it."
Hebrews 12:11 (NIV)

It is not easy to live life with an "I've Decided" mindset instead of an "I'll Try" mindset. As scripture says, it can seem painful at times. It's difficult because it requires change. You have to go into strict training and work hard to create a new groove for your mind to follow. This develops your discipline, which is needed in order to be successful in your goals and dreams. The fifth step in changing your mindset from I'll try to an I've decided mindset is to develop discipline.

The most awesome thing about developing discipline is the fruit of righteousness that it yields to people who have been trained by it. I believe this is the peace that comes from deep within to those who live with an "I've Decided" mindset. When we give in to those temptations and learned behaviors or habits that seem pleasant at the time but go against our deepest desires, goals, and dreams, we miss out on the ultimate victory, which is success.

7. EXCEL

The **E** in DECIDE is to **Excel** in the result.

Yes, the sixth step is to excel! This final step makes the other five steps well worth the hard work. This is the fruit of righteousness where you can feel peace knowing you have successfully completed your goal. Your hard work has officially paid off, and you are reaping what you've sown.

The word "excel" means to be exceptionally good at or proficient in an activity or subject. Whatever behavior you needed to change or task you needed to complete to achieve your goal, you are now exceptionally proficient at it.

Did you know that it glorifies God for you to successfully achieve your goals?

"This is to my Father's glory, that you bear much fruit, showing yourselves to be my disciples." - John 15:8 (NIV)

God wants you to be successful, and He has already prepared the way for you to succeed in every goal or desire He has placed in your heart.

"being confident of this, that he who began a good work in you will carry it on to completion until the day of Christ Jesus." - Philippians 1:6 (NIV)

8. 6 STEPS TO SUCCESS-RECAP

You are now equipped with all six steps to successfully complete your goals and dreams. Whatever it is you desire to do, you can apply the DECIDE methodology of behavioral change and excel in the end result.

Let's recap:

Whatever your goal or dream is, you need to apply I've decided to the beginning of it.

I've decided to…

_____

because I can!

Once you have decided on your goal, you are ready to begin going through each step which will move you toward the finish line of success.

- The first step is to **Declare** your goal.

- The second step is to **Envision** your goal.

- The third step is to **Cultivate** a mindset that the emotion follows the action.

- The fourth step is to **Incorporate** your "why," or X-factor, for wanting to accomplish the goal, the right people of influence, and the resources and assets you need

- The fifth step is to **Develop Discipline.**

- The sixth step is to **Excel** in the end result.

DECIDE

A 6 Step Behavioral Change Methodology that works

The 6 steps to Success:

1. **Declare-**

2. **Envision-**

3. **Cultivate-**

4. **Incorporate-**

5. **Develop Discipline-**

6. **Excel-**

Bonus:

**I've Decided Weekly Motivational Journal
"6 Steps to Success!"**

This Journal Belongs to:

_____

I've decided to:

_____

**It's not easy. It's hard!
If it were easy, everyone would do it!**

I've decided to...

_____

_____

_____

because I can!

Declare:

Who will I share my goals with this week?

Envision:

Draw or paste pictures that represent your goals and capture images of your future self successfully completing your goals as well as images that represent the outcome if you don't achieve success.

Cultivate: What is one positive change you can make this week and a thought you can take captive to align to this change?

Incorporate: What is your "why" behind your goal or your X-factor? Who are your people of influence, and what are your resources and assets?

Develop Discipline: What is the one area in which you can practice discipline this week?

Excel: What is your desired outcome?

You don't have to be great to start, but you have to start to be great!

I've decided to…

_____

_____

_____

because I can!

Declare:

Who will I share my goals with this week?

Envision:

Draw or paste pictures that represent your goals and capture images of your future self successfully completing your goals as well as images that represent the outcome if you don't achieve success.

Cultivate: What is one positive change you can make this week, and a thought you can take captive to align to this change?

Incorporate: What is your "why" behind your goal or your X-factor? Who are your people of influence, and what are your resources and assets?

Develop Discipline: What is the one area in which you can practice discipline this week?

Excel: What is your desired outcome?

You are going to reach your goal!

I've decided to...

_____

_____

_____

because I can!

Declare:

Who will I share my goals with this week?

Envision:

Draw or paste pictures that represent your goals and capture images of your future self successfully completing your goals as well as images that represent the outcome if you don't achieve success.

Cultivate: What is one positive change you can make this week, and a thought you can take captive to align to this change?

Incorporate: What is your "why" behind your goal or your X-factor? Who are your people of influence, and what are your resources and assets?

Develop Discipline: What is the one area in which you can practice discipline this week?

Excel: What is your desired outcome?

If you can dream it, you can do it!

I've decided to…

_____

_____

_____

because I can!

Declare:
Who will I share my goals with this week?

Envision:
Draw or paste pictures that represent your goals and capture images of your future self successfully completing your goals as well as images that represent the outcome if you don't achieve success.

Cultivate: What is one positive change you can make this week, and a thought you can take captive to align to this change?

Incorporate: What is your "why" behind your goal or your X-factor? Who are your people of influence, and what are your resources and assets?

Develop Discipline: What is the one area in which you can practice discipline this week?

Excel: What is your desired outcome?

The time is now. Tomorrow is not promised!

I've decided to...

_____

_____

_____

because I can!

Declare:

Who will I share my goals with this week?

Envision:

Draw or paste pictures that represent your goals and capture images of your future self successfully completing your goals as well as images that represent the outcome if you don't achieve success.

Cultivate: What is one positive change you can make this week, and a thought you can take captive to align to this change?

Incorporate: What is your "why" behind your goal or your X-factor? Who are your people of influence, and what are your resources and assets?

Develop Discipline: What is the one area in which you can practice discipline this week?

Excel: What is your desired outcome?

I've decided to...

_____

_____

_____

because I can!

Declare:

Who will I share my goals with this week?

Envision:

Draw or paste pictures that represent your goals and capture images of your future self successfully completing your goals as well as images that represent the outcome if you don't achieve success.

Cultivate: What is one positive change you can make this week, and a thought you can take captive to align to this change?

Incorporate: What is your "why" behind your goal or your X-factor? Who are your people of influence, and what are your resources and assets?

Develop Discipline: What is the one area in which you can practice discipline this week?

Excel: What is your desired outcome?

I've decided to...

_____

_____

_____

because I can!

Declare:
Who will I share my goals with this week?

Envision:
Draw or paste pictures that represent your goals and capture images of your future self successfully completing your goals as well as images that represent the outcome if you don't achieve success.

Cultivate: What is one positive change you can make this week, and a thought you can take captive to align to this change?

Incorporate: What is your "why" behind your goal or your X-factor? Who are your people of influence, and what are your resources and assets?

Develop Discipline: What is the one area in which you can practice discipline this week?

Excel: What is your desired outcome?

Don't Stop! People are watching.

I've decided to...

_____

_____

_____

because I can!

Declare:
Who will I share my goals with this week?

Envision:
Draw or paste pictures that represent your goals and capture images of your future self successfully completing your goals as well as images that represent the outcome if you don't achieve success.

Cultivate: What is one positive change you can make this week, and a thought you can take captive to align to this change?

Incorporate: What is your "why" behind your goal or your X-factor? Who are your people of influence, and what are your resources and assets?

Develop Discipline: What is the one area in which you can practice discipline this week?

Excel: What is your desired outcome?

Stay Focused!

I've decided to...

_____

_____

_____

because I can!

Declare:
Who will I share my goals with this week?

Envision:
Draw or paste pictures that represent your goals and capture images of your future self successfully completing your goals as well as images that represent the outcome if you don't achieve success.

Cultivate: What is one positive change you can make this week, and a thought you can take captive to align to this change?

Incorporate: What is your "why" behind your goal or your X-factor? Who are your people of influence, and what are your resources and assets?

Develop Discipline: What is the one area in which you can practice discipline this week?

Excel: What is your desired outcome?

Tell yourself: I can do this!

I've decided to...

_____

_____

_____

because I can!

Declare:
Who will I share my goals with this week?

Envision:
Draw or paste pictures that represent your goals and capture images of your future self successfully completing your goals as well as images that represent the outcome if you don't achieve success.

Cultivate: What is one positive change you can make this week, and a thought you can take captive to align to this change?

Incorporate: What is your "why" behind your goal or your X-factor? Who are your people of influence, and what are your resources and assets?

Develop Discipline: What is the one area in which you can practice discipline this week?

Excel: What is your desired outcome?

Believe in yourself!

I've decided to...

_____

_____

_____

because I can!

Declare:

Who will I share my goals with this week?

Envision:

Draw or paste pictures that represent your goals and capture images of your future self successfully completing your goals as well as images that represent the outcome if you don't achieve success.

Cultivate: What is one positive change you can make this week, and a thought you can take captive to align to this change?

Incorporate: What is your "why" behind your goal or your X-factor? Who are your people of influence, and what are your resources and assets?

Develop Discipline: What is the one area in which you can practice discipline this week?

Excel: What is your desired outcome?

Break through the wall!

I've decided to...

_____

_____

_____

because I can!

Declare:

Who will I share my goals with this week?

Envision:

Draw or paste pictures that represent your goals and capture images of your future self successfully completing your goals as well as images that represent the outcome if you don't achieve success.

Cultivate: What is one positive change you can make this week, and a thought you can take captive to align to this change?

Incorporate: What is your "why" behind your goal or your X-factor? Who are your people of influence, and what are your resources and assets?

Develop Discipline: What is the one area in which you can practice discipline this week?

Excel: What is your desired outcome?

I've decided to...

_____

_____

_____

because I can!

Declare:
Who will I share my goals with this week?

Envision:
Draw or paste pictures that represent your goals and capture images of your future self successfully completing your goals as well as images that represent the outcome if you don't achieve success.

Cultivate: What is one positive change you can make this week, and a thought you can take captive to align to this change?

Incorporate: What is your "why" behind your goal or your X-factor? Who are your people of influence, and what are your resources and assets?

Develop Discipline: What is the one area in which you can practice discipline this week?

Excel: What is your desired outcome?

Way to go!

I've decided to...

_____

_____

_____

because I can!

Declare:
Who will I share my goals with this week?

Envision:
Draw or paste pictures that represent your goals and capture images of your future self successfully completing your goals as well as images that represent the outcome if you don't achieve success.

Cultivate: What is one positive change you can make this week, and a thought you can take captive to align to this change?

Incorporate: What is your "why" behind your goal or your X-factor? Who are your people of influence, and what are your resources and assets?

Develop Discipline: What is the one area in which you can practice discipline this week?

Excel: What is your desired outcome?

Don't look back!

I've decided to...

_____

_____

_____

because I can!

Declare:

Who will I share my goals with this week?

Envision:

Draw or paste pictures that represent your goals and capture images of your future self successfully completing your goals as well as images that represent the outcome if you don't achieve success.

Cultivate: What is one positive change you can make this week, and a thought you can take captive to align to this change?

Incorporate: What is your "why" behind your goal or your X-factor? Who are your people of influence, and what are your resources and assets?

Develop Discipline: What is the one area in which you can practice discipline this week?

Excel: What is your desired outcome?

You are ahead of anyone who hasn't started their goal yet!

I've decided to...

_____

_____

_____

because I can!

Declare:

Who will I share my goals with this week?

Envision:

Draw or paste pictures that represent your goals and capture images of your future self successfully completing your goals as well as images that represent the outcome if you don't achieve success.

Cultivate: What is one positive change you can make this week, and a thought you can take captive to align to this change?

Incorporate: What is your "why" behind your goal or your X-factor? Who are your people of influence, and what are your resources and assets?

Develop Discipline: What is the one area in which you can practice discipline this week?

Excel: What is your desired outcome?

If you do what you've always done, you will get what you've always gotten!

I've decided to…

_____

_____

_____

because I can!

Declare:
Who will I share my goals with this week?

Envision:
Draw or paste pictures that represent your goals and capture images of your future self successfully completing your goals as well as images that represent the outcome if you don't achieve success.

Cultivate: What is one positive change you can make this week, and a thought you can take captive to align to this change?

Incorporate: What is your "why" behind your goal or your X-factor? Who are your people of influence, and what are your resources and assets?

Develop Discipline: What is the one area in which you can practice discipline this week?

Excel: What is your desired outcome?

Give up the good, and go for the great!

I've decided to...

_____

_____

_____

because I can!

Declare:

Who will I share my goals with this week?

Envision:

Draw or paste pictures that represent your goals and capture images of your future self successfully completing your goals as well as images that represent the outcome if you don't achieve success.

Cultivate: What is one positive change you can make this week, and a thought you can take captive to align to this change?

Incorporate: What is your "why" behind your goal or your X-factor? Who are your people of influence, and what are your resources and assets?

Develop Discipline: What is the one area in which you can practice discipline this week?

Excel: What is your desired outcome?

I've decided to...

_____
_____
_____

                              because I can!

Declare:
Who will I share my goals with this week?

Envision:
Draw or paste pictures that represent your goals and capture images of your future self successfully completing your goals as well as images that represent the outcome if you don't achieve success.

Cultivate: What is one positive change you can make this week, and a thought you can take captive to align to this change?

Incorporate: What is your "why" behind your goal or your X-factor? Who are your people of influence, and what are your resources and assets?

Develop Discipline: What is the one area in which you can practice discipline this week?

Excel: What is your desired outcome?

Say these words out loud: I am awesome!

I've decided to...

_____

_____

_____

because I can!

Declare:
Who will I share my goals with this week?

Envision:
Draw or paste pictures that represent your goals and capture images of your future self successfully completing your goals as well as images that represent the outcome if you don't achieve success.

Cultivate: What is one positive change you can make this week, and a thought you can take captive to align to this change?

Incorporate: What is your "why" behind your goal or your X-factor? Who are your people of influence, and what are your resources and assets?

Develop Discipline: What is the one area in which you can practice discipline this week?

Excel: What is your desired outcome?

Impossible is a lie!

I've decided to...

_____

_____

_____

because I can!

Declare:

Who will I share my goals with this week?

Envision:

Draw or paste pictures that represent your goals and capture images of your future self successfully completing your goals as well as images that represent the outcome if you don't achieve success.

Cultivate: What is one positive change you can make this week, and a thought you can take captive to align to this change?

Incorporate: What is your "why" behind your goal or your X-factor? Who are your people of influence, and what are your resources and assets?

Develop Discipline: What is the one area in which you can practice discipline this week?

Excel: What is your desired outcome?

Success is the sum of small efforts!

I've decided to...

_____

_____

_____

because I can!

Declare:
Who will I share my goals with this week?

Envision:
Draw or paste pictures that represent your goals and capture images of your future self successfully completing your goals as well as images that represent the outcome if you don't achieve success.

Cultivate: What is one positive change you can make this week, and a thought you can take captive to align to this change?

Incorporate: What is your "why" behind your goal or your X-factor? Who are your people of influence, and what are your resources and assets?

Develop Discipline: What is the one area in which you can practice discipline this week?

Excel: What is your desired outcome?

Never, ever give up!

I've decided to...

_____

_____

_____

because I can!

Declare:
Who will I share my goals with this week?

Envision:
Draw or paste pictures that represent your goals and capture images of your future self successfully completing your goals as well as images that represent the outcome if you don't achieve success.

Cultivate: What is one positive change you can make this week, and a thought you can take captive to align to this change?

Incorporate: What is your "why" behind your goal or your X-factor? Who are your people of influence, and what are your resources and assets?

Develop Discipline: What is the one area in which you can practice discipline this week?

Excel: What is your desired outcome?

Be strong and courageous!

I've decided to…

____

____

____

because I can!

Declare:

Who will I share my goals with this week?

Envision:

Draw or paste pictures that represent your goals and capture images of your future self successfully completing your goals as well as images that represent the outcome if you don't achieve success.

Cultivate: What is one positive change you can make this week, and a thought you can take captive to align to this change?

Incorporate: What is your "why" behind your goal or your X-factor? Who are your people of influence, and what are your resources and assets?

Develop Discipline: What is the one area in which you can practice discipline this week?

Excel: What is your desired outcome?

Mistakes are proof that you are in action!

I've decided to...

_____

_____

_____

because I can!

Declare:
Who will I share my goals with this week?

Envision:
Draw or paste pictures that represent your goals and capture images of your future self successfully completing your goals as well as images that represent the outcome if you don't achieve success.

Cultivate: What is one positive change you can make this week, and a thought you can take captive to align to this change?

Incorporate: What is your "why" behind your goal or your X-factor? Who are your people of influence, and what are your resources and assets?

Develop Discipline: What is the one area in which you can practice discipline this week?

Excel: What is your desired outcome?

With hard work, there are no limits!

I've decided to...

_____

_____

_____

because I can!

Declare:
Who will I share my goals with this week?

Envision:
Draw or paste pictures that represent your goals and capture images of your future self successfully completing your goals as well as images that represent the outcome if you don't achieve success.

Cultivate: What is one positive change you can make this week, and a thought you can take captive to align to this change?

Incorporate: What is your "why" behind your goal or your X-factor? Who are your people of influence, and what are your resources and assets?

Develop Discipline: What is the one area in which you can practice discipline this week?

Excel: What is your desired outcome?

Don't stop now!

I've decided to...

_____

_____

_____

because I can!

Declare:
Who will I share my goals with this week?

Envision:
Draw or paste pictures that represent your goals and capture images of your future self successfully completing your goals as well as images that represent the outcome if you don't achieve success.

Cultivate: What is one positive change you can make this week, and a thought you can take captive to align to this change?

Incorporate: What is your "why" behind your goal or your X-factor? Who are your people of influence, and what are your resources and assets?

Develop Discipline: What is the one area in which you can practice discipline this week?

Excel: What is your desired outcome?

You are closer to your goal than yesterday!

I've decided to…

---

because I can!

Declare:

Who will I share my goals with this week?

Envision:

Draw or paste pictures that represent your goals and capture images of your future self successfully completing your goals as well as images that represent the outcome if you don't achieve success.

Cultivate: What is one positive change you can make this week, and a thought you can take captive to align to this change?

Incorporate: What is your "why" behind your goal or your X-factor? Who are your people of influence, and what are your resources and assets?

Develop Discipline: What is the one area in which you can practice discipline this week?

Excel: What is your desired outcome?

You were born for greatness!

I've decided to...

_____
_____
_____

because I can!

Declare:
Who will I share my goals with this week?

Envision:
Draw or paste pictures that represent your goals and capture images of your future self successfully completing your goals as well as images that represent the outcome if you don't achieve success.

Cultivate: What is one positive change you can make this week, and a thought you can take captive to align to this change?

Incorporate: What is your "why" behind your goal or your X-factor? Who are your people of influence, and what are your resources and assets?

Develop Discipline: What is the one area in which you can practice discipline this week?

Excel: What is your desired outcome?

I've decided to...

_____
_____
_____

because I can!

Declare:

Who will I share my goals with this week?

Envision:

Draw or paste pictures that represent your goals and capture images of your future self successfully completing your goals as well as images that represent the outcome if you don't achieve success.

Cultivate: What is one positive change you can make this week, and a thought you can take captive to align to this change?

Incorporate: What is your "why" behind your goal or your X-factor? Who are your people of influence, and what are your resources and assets?

Develop Discipline: What is the one area in which you can practice discipline this week?

Excel: What is your desired outcome?

This is by far your best victory!

I've decided to...

_____

_____

_____

because I can!

Declare:
Who will I share my goals with this week?

Envision:
Draw or paste pictures that represent your goals and capture images of your future self successfully completing your goals as well as images that represent the outcome if you don't achieve success.

Cultivate: What is one positive change you can make this week, and a thought you can take captive to align to this change?

Incorporate: What is your "why" behind your goal or your X-factor? Who are your people of influence, and what are your resources and assets?

Develop Discipline: What is the one area in which you can practice discipline this week?

Excel: What is your desired outcome?

Stop when you're done, not when you're tired!

I've decided to…

_____

_____

_____

because I can!

Declare:
Who will I share my goals with this week?

Envision:
Draw or paste pictures that represent your goals and capture images of your future self successfully completing your goals as well as images that represent the outcome if you don't achieve success.

Cultivate: What is one positive change you can make this week, and a thought you can take captive to align to this change?

Incorporate: What is your "why" behind your goal or your X-factor? Who are your people of influence, and what are your resources and assets?

Develop Discipline: What is the one area in which you can practice discipline this week?

Excel: What is your desired outcome?

Nothing great comes easily!

I've decided to...

_____

_____

_____

because I can!

Declare:
Who will I share my goals with this week?

Envision:
Draw or paste pictures that represent your goals and capture images of your future self successfully completing your goals as well as images that represent the outcome if you don't achieve success.

Cultivate: What is one positive change you can make this week, and a thought you can take captive to align to this change?

Incorporate: What is your "why" behind your goal or your X-factor? Who are your people of influence, and what are your resources and assets?

Develop Discipline: What is the one area in which you can practice discipline this week?

Excel: What is your desired outcome?

Thinking about stopping? Work harder!

I've decided to...

_____

_____

_____

because I can!

Declare:

Who will I share my goals with this week?

Envision:

Draw or paste pictures that represent your goals and capture images of your future self successfully completing your goals as well as images that represent the outcome if you don't achieve success.

Cultivate: What is one positive change you can make this week, and a thought you can take captive to align to this change?

Incorporate: What is your "why" behind your goal or your X-factor? Who are your people of influence, and what are your resources and assets?

Develop Discipline: What is the one area in which you can practice discipline this week?

Excel: What is your desired outcome?

The best is yet to come!

I've decided to...

_____

_____

_____

because I can!

Declare:

Who will I share my goals with this week?

Envision:

Draw or paste pictures that represent your goals and capture images of your future self successfully completing your goals as well as images that represent the outcome if you don't achieve success.

Cultivate: What is one positive change you can make this week, and a thought you can take captive to align to this change?

Incorporate: What is your "why" behind your goal or your X-factor? Who are your people of influence, and what are your resources and assets?

Develop Discipline: What is the one area in which you can practice discipline this week?

Excel: What is your desired outcome?

Don't wait for things to happen. Make them happen!

I've decided to...

_____

_____

_____

because I can!

Declare:
Who will I share my goals with this week?

Envision:
Draw or paste pictures that represent your goals and capture images of your future self successfully completing your goals as well as images that represent the outcome if you don't achieve success.

Cultivate: What is one positive change you can make this week, and a thought you can take captive to align to this change?

Incorporate: What is your "why" behind your goal or your X-factor? Who are your people of influence, and what are your resources and assets?

Develop Discipline: What is the one area in which you can practice discipline this week?

Excel: What is your desired outcome?

Successful people never worry about what other people are doing!

I've decided to…

_____

_____

_____

because I can!

Declare:

Who will I share my goals with this week?

Envision:

Draw or paste pictures that represent your goals and capture images of your future self successfully completing your goals as well as images that represent the outcome if you don't achieve success.

Cultivate: What is one positive change you can make this week, and a thought you can take captive to align to this change?

Incorporate: What is your "why" behind your goal or your X-factor? Who are your people of influence, and what are your resources and assets?

Develop Discipline: What is the one area in which you can practice discipline this week?

Excel: What is your desired outcome?

Focus on change, and the results will come!

I've decided to...

_____

_____

_____

because I can!

Declare:

Who will I share my goals with this week?

Envision:

Draw or paste pictures that represent your goals and capture images of your future self successfully completing your goals as well as images that represent the outcome if you don't achieve success.

Cultivate: What is one positive change you can make this week, and a thought you can take captive to align to this change?

Incorporate: What is your "why" behind your goal or your X-factor? Who are your people of influence, and what are your resources and assets?

Develop Discipline: What is the one area in which you can practice discipline this week?

Excel: What is your desired outcome?

Go the extra mile!

I've decided to...

_____

_____

_____

because I can!

Declare:

Who will I share my goals with this week?

Envision:

Draw or paste pictures that represent your goals and capture images of your future self successfully completing your goals as well as images that represent the outcome if you don't achieve success.

Cultivate: What is one positive change you can make this week, and a thought you can take captive to align to this change?

Incorporate: What is your "why" behind your goal or your X-factor? Who are your people of influence, and what are your resources and assets?

Develop Discipline: What is the one area in which you can practice discipline this week?

Excel: What is your desired outcome?

At mile twenty, the marathon begins!

I've decided to...

_____

_____

_____

because I can!

Declare:

Who will I share my goals with this week?

Envision:

Draw or paste pictures that represent your goals and capture images of your future self successfully completing your goals as well as images that represent the outcome if you don't achieve success.

Cultivate: What is one positive change you can make this week, and a thought you can take captive to align to this change?

Incorporate: What is your "why" behind your goal or your X-factor? Who are your people of influence, and what are your resources and assets?

Develop Discipline: What is the one area in which you can practice discipline this week?

Excel: What is your desired outcome?

There are no shortcuts to success!

I've decided to...

_____

_____

_____

because I can!

Declare:

Who will I share my goals with this week?

Envision:

Draw or paste pictures that represent your goals and capture images of your future self successfully completing your goals as well as images that represent the outcome if you don't achieve success.

Cultivate: What is one positive change you can make this week, and a thought you can take captive to align to this change?

Incorporate: What is your "why" behind your goal or your X-factor? Who are your people of influence, and what are your resources and assets?

Develop Discipline: What is the one area in which you can practice discipline this week?

Excel: What is your desired outcome?

Act like the person you want to become!

I've decided to…

_____

_____

_____

because I can!

Declare:

Who will I share my goals with this week?

Envision:

Draw or paste pictures that represent your goals and capture images of your future self successfully completing your goals as well as images that represent the outcome if you don't achieve success.

Cultivate: What is one positive change you can make this week, and a thought you can take captive to align to this change?

Incorporate: What is your "why" behind your goal or your X-factor? Who are your people of influence, and what are your resources and assets?

Develop Discipline: What is the one area in which you can practice discipline this week?

Excel: What is your desired outcome?

It's only a wall. Climb over it!

I've decided to...

_____

_____

because I can!

Declare:

Who will I share my goals with this week?

Envision:

Draw or paste pictures that represent your goals and capture images of your future self successfully completing your goals as well as images that represent the outcome if you don't achieve success.

Cultivate: What is one positive change you can make this week, and a thought you can take captive to align to this change?

Incorporate: What is your "why" behind your goal or your X-factor? Who are your people of influence, and what are your resources and assets?

Develop Discipline: What is the one area in which you can practice discipline this week?

Excel: What is your desired outcome?

Wherever you go, there you are!

I've decided to...

_____

_____

_____

because I can!

Declare:

Who will I share my goals with this week?

Envision:

Draw or paste pictures that represent your goals and capture images of your future self successfully completing your goals as well as images that represent the outcome if you don't achieve success.

Cultivate: What is one positive change you can make this week, and a thought you can take captive to align to this change?

Incorporate: What is your "why" behind your goal or your X-factor? Who are your people of influence, and what are your resources and assets?

Develop Discipline: What is the one area in which you can practice discipline this week?

Excel: What is your desired outcome?

Today is a new day. Rise up and start fresh!

I've decided to…

_____

_____

_____

because I can!

Declare:

Who will I share my goals with this week?

Envision:

Draw or paste pictures that represent your goals and capture images of your future self successfully completing your goals as well as images that represent the outcome if you don't achieve success.

Cultivate: What is one positive change you can make this week, and a thought you can take captive to align to this change?

Incorporate: What is your "why" behind your goal or your X-factor? Who are your people of influence, and what are your resources and assets?

Develop Discipline: What is the one area in which you can practice discipline this week?

Excel: What is your desired outcome?

Keep your eye on the prize!

I've decided to...

_____

_____

_____

because I can!

Declare:

Who will I share my goals with this week?

Envision:

Draw or paste pictures that represent your goals and capture images of your future self successfully completing your goals as well as images that represent the outcome if you don't achieve success.

Cultivate: What is one positive change you can make this week, and a thought you can take captive to align to this change?

Incorporate: What is your "why" behind your goal or your X-factor? Who are your people of influence, and what are your resources and assets?

Develop Discipline: What is the one area in which you can practice discipline this week?

Excel: What is your desired outcome?

Don't be the same. Be better!

I've decided to...

_____

_____

_____

because I can!

Declare:

Who will I share my goals with this week?

Envision:

Draw or paste pictures that represent your goals and capture images of your future self successfully completing your goals as well as images that represent the outcome if you don't achieve success.

Cultivate: What is one positive change you can make this week, and a thought you can take captive to align to this change?

Incorporate: What is your "why" behind your goal or your X-factor? Who are your people of influence, and what are your resources and assets?

Develop Discipline: What is the one area in which you can practice discipline this week?

Excel: What is your desired outcome?

You are so close!

I've decided to...

_____

_____

_____

because I can!

Declare:

Who will I share my goals with this week?

Envision:

Draw or paste pictures that represent your goals and capture images of your future self successfully completing your goals as well as images that represent the outcome if you don't achieve success.

Cultivate: What is one positive change you can make this week, and a thought you can take captive to align to this change?

Incorporate: What is your "why" behind your goal or your X-factor? Who are your people of influence, and what are your resources and assets?

Develop Discipline: What is the one area in which you can practice discipline this week?

Excel: What is your desired outcome?

Think about why you started!

I've decided to...

_____

_____

_____

because I can!

Declare:

Who will I share my goals with this week?

Envision:

Draw or paste pictures that represent your goals and capture images of your future self successfully completing your goals as well as images that represent the outcome if you don't achieve success.

Cultivate: What is one positive change you can make this week, and a thought you can take captive to align to this change?

Incorporate: What is your "why" behind your goal or your X-factor? Who are your people of influence, and what are your resources and assets?

Develop Discipline: What is the one area in which you can practice discipline this week?

Excel: What is your desired outcome?

You are making things happen!

I've decided to...

_____

_____

_____

because I can!

Declare:

Who will I share my goals with this week?

Envision:

Draw or paste pictures that represent your goals and capture images of your future self successfully completing your goals as well as images that represent the outcome if you don't achieve success.

Cultivate: What is one positive change you can make this week, and a thought you can take captive to align to this change?

Incorporate: What is your "why" behind your goal or your X-factor? Who are your people of influence, and what are your resources and assets?

Develop Discipline: What is the one area in which you can practice discipline this week?

Excel: What is your desired outcome?

Success is just around the corner!

I've decided to...

_____

_____

_____

because I can!

Declare:
Who will I share my goals with this week?

Envision:
Draw or paste pictures that represent your goals and capture images of your future self successfully completing your goals as well as images that represent the outcome if you don't achieve success.

Cultivate: What is one positive change you can make this week, and a thought you can take captive to align to this change?

Incorporate: What is your "why" behind your goal or your X-factor? Who are your people of influence, and what are your resources and assets?

Develop Discipline: What is the one area in which you can practice discipline this week?

Excel: What is your desired outcome?

You have excelled in your goal and crossed the finish line. Victory is yours!

Kim Martin

Highlights:

_____
_____
_____
_____
_____
_____
_____
_____
_____
_____
_____
_____
_____
_____
_____
_____

Challenges:

_____
_____
_____
_____
_____
_____
_____
_____
_____
_____
_____
_____
_____
_____
_____
_____

"Do you not know that in a race all the runners run, but only one gets the prize? Run in such a way as to get the prize."

1 Corinthians 9:24 (NIV)

ABOUT THE AUTHOR

Kim Martin has been a business owner of Curves since January 18th, 1999. What she loves most about her career is having the opportunity to witness the amazing and lifesaving transformation of her members who are achieving their fitness and weight goals.

Kim has over twenty years of experience in her field and is certified in Nutrition, Exercise Kinesiology, and Behavior Management. She loves to teach, motivate, and inspire people to be better and has been speaking to audiences for more than fifteen years.

In September of 2014 Kim "decided" to use the experience she has of operating her own franchise business, marketing skills, and ability to motivate others, and begin a startup business, I've Decided. This unique marketing company is designed to inspire and motivate people to make a positive lifestyle choice or fulfill a dream. The community-wide effort of personal improvement will impact positive change throughout any city and brand the business members as community-wide difference makers.

Kim is very involved in her community and nonprofit organizations, such as St Jude, Susan G. Komen, Southside Mission, and PUP. She is a member of the National Association of Women Business Owners, Women in Leadership, and the Peoria Chamber of Commerce.

She has been awarded Franchisee of the Year and Multiple Franchisee of the Year by Curves International, and her Curves in Peoria is considered to be one of the top twenty clubs in our nation.

What she is most proud of is her family. Kim is married to Joe Martin, and together, as a blended family, they have seven awesome children. They love their crazy life!

Made in the USA
Columbia, SC
07 January 2020